101
"I AM"
Power
Affirmations.

Tony T Robinson.

Copyright © 20

Author, Tony T Robinson

Title, 101 "I AM" Power Affirmations

© 2014, Tony T Robinson

© All rights Reserved.

*

Tony T Robinson

DEDICATION

*

I would like to dedicate this book to YOU and to anyone who does not yet truly believe in their innate beauty and greatness but has enough hope and faith in themselves to be the best version of themselves that they can be and that the affirmations contained within this book will help to improve your self-esteem self-worth and confidence.

Affirmations helped me climb out of a dark hole that I realised was my own creation. It was my creation because my internal language was destructive and based on negative self-speak and negative affirmations. I learned that what I said about myself created the reality I lived in. By simply changing what I said and how I thought about myself I was able to transform my life to the point where I am now in a position to help other people transform their lives.

I would also like to thank my friends and family who have been with me every step of the way and I offer my deepest gratitude for their support in this new chapter of my life.

Love always.

Tony T.

*

CONTENTS

101

"I AM" Power

Affirmations.

"I am" are the two most powerful words known to man because whatever you say after them will determine how you think and feel about yourself.

They influence your ability to function in the world and the quality of the future that you create for yourself and for the people you invite into your world because your words create your reality.

It is important to make certain that you are creating a life and a way of living that you truly want and deserve, not only for yourself but for your friends family and for generations to come that may never know you personally but will grow up in the legacy you leave behind.

What makes this book unique and different from all the other affirmation books is that all 101 Affirmations begin with "I AM". This supercharges each affirmation with additional power because when you say those two words you are directly addressing the core of yourself. You are not talking about something "out there" in the ether, instead you are connecting to something "in here" which is deep inside your unconscious or your soul and that has life changing consequences.

"I AM" is the essence of who you are! Whatever you say after that will either greatly improve the quality of your life or quickly diminish it. If there is something that you want to change or improve in your life using an affirmation that begins with I AM will help to facilitate that change more quickly and at a deeper level.

"I AM" not only determines how you think and feel about yourself but it is how the rest of the world learns how to relate to you. Whatever you say after "I AM" educates them in how they should treat you because you are setting the example for them to follow. So you had better make sure it is a good example.

If you find that other people are treating you disrespectfully or are rude and demeaning to you then stop and check yourself for a second. Ask "What am I saying about myself that allows them to think that what they are saying or doing is acceptable?"

Are you responsible for creating the dynamic that is operating in your life right now? Have you created healthy boundaries because if you have not it will be very easy for other people to take advantage of that and exploit your fears and insecurities for their benefits.

Remember people will only treat you as badly as you allow them to!

Negative Affirmations.

It's quite possible that you are using or have used a form of negative affirmations. Negative affirmations not only disrespect you but diminishes your confidence and self-worth and advertises to the rest of the world that it is ok for them to treat you badly.

A negative "I AM" affirmation can be any of the following –

- I am so stupid.
- I am such a fool.
- I am always getting things wrong.
- I am so unlucky, nothing ever works for me.
- I am so fat and I hate my body.
- I am so ugly and I hate the way I look.
- I am so useless and I just don't know what to do.
- I am never going to find real love, who could ever love me?
- I am such a bad person and nothing good ever happens to me.
- I am always being taken advantage of and used by other people.

(This is by no means an exhaustive list) but I am sure some of these sound familiar to you and these are only the ones that begin with "I AM" this does not include the countless other forms of negative affirmations that you may say without even realising it.

It can be very easy to slip into a negative way of relating to yourself. It may have begun as a child especially if you were reprimanded or "put down" by your parents/family or other children at school or even as you got older by boyfriends or girlfriends etc.

If this pattern of thinking begins early enough it becomes so ingrained into your personality that you barely even notice that you think and speak negatively about yourself. This becomes your pathology (the way you think).

Negative affirmations not only reinforce how you feel about yourself but they can also create low self-esteem, a lack of confidence, depression or suicidal thoughts and sometimes suicide attempts because every time you say or think a negative thought you are telling yourself that you are bad, that you are useless, that you are worthless and if that is what you are saying about yourself then it stands to reason that you are going to believe those thoughts and those words because they come from you. The good news is that cycle can be broken and YOU have the power to break it.

The first step in changing your pathology is identifying your negative self-speak. Take a note pad and every time you hear yourself saying or thinking a negative affirmation write it down. It may take a little while to realise what you are saying about yourself but the more you do it the easier it will be to recognise. If you need help doing this you could always ask someone close to you to point out when you use negative self-speak; they are probably already aware of the language you use to describe yourself and may have already pointed it out to you in the past.

Once you have written your list of negative affirmations you will have brought unconscious thoughts and patterns into a state of consciousness. This enables you to be more alert and aware of what you are saying and when you are saying it so that you can begin to implement a new positive way of relating to yourself.

When you become conscious of your thinking you can start to establish control over those thoughts and this will help to change old destructive habits. Having awareness of what you say and the situations in which you say them will help you to stop and implement a new positive version of the old destructive thought.

In order to truly change how you think and feel about yourself it is important to replace the identified negative affirmations with new Positive Affirmations. Refer back to your pad, take each negative affirmation and cross it through and then create a positive alternative.

With your new list of powerful affirmations, each time you find yourself saying the negative version repeat the positive counterpart for at least one minute to balance its negative effect.

The more you do this the greater the positive influence will be until eventually the positive affirmation becomes your auto response, once this happens you know you have reconditioned your thinking.

Here are a couple of examples of how to create new positive affirmations to replace the old negative ones.

<u>Negative Affirmation.</u>

"I am so useless I will never get that job"

<u>Positive version</u>

"I am smart and capable and I deserve to get that job"

Or

<u>Negative affirmation.</u>

"I'm so ugly nobody will ever like me.

<u>Positive Version</u>

"I am attractive and I deserve to have love in my life"

I have found there are several main areas in our lives that benefit from the use of Positive Affirmations and I have organised this book into the following categories.

- Self-Esteem Affirmations (general)
- I AM a good person.
- Affirmations for Confidence.
- Affirmations for Success.
- Inner Strength Affirmations.
- Responsibility Affirmations.
- Gratitude Affirmations
- Health and Fitness Affirmations
- Love Affirmations.

Although I have organised the book into particular sections there are many ways that you can use the affirmations but you need to find what works best for you so here are a few suggestions that you may find helpful.

- You can work through the book starting at the beginning focusing on one affirmation per day until you reach the end.

- There may be a particular area of your life right now where you need to focus and so you can concentrate on that group of affirmations.

- You can choose an affirmation at random and use that as your daily theme.

- Take one affirmation from each section each day so that you improve all the different areas of your life on a regular basis.

- Find your favourite affirmations and create your own daily list.

I'm sure there are other variations you can use but what is important is that you find whatever is enjoyable for you.

In order to maximise their effect I would limit your list to no more than 10 affirmations in any one day so that your unconscious mind can start to absorb the new positive messages and not be overloaded.

Perhaps there is a specific affirmation that suits a time of day, i.e. in the morning or evening or there may be one that is relevant to a specific situation where you need to feel confident. You may need to use a specific Health and Diet affirmation at every meal time in order to feel in control of your diet.

Regardless of how you use affirmations it is important to remember that they have the power to change your life and the way you think about yourself.

How to use Affirmations.

There are several ways to use affirmations such as-

- Reading and re-reading them to yourself.
- Reading them aloud.
- Writing them down.
- Record them and play them out loud.
- Mirror work.

Reading Affirmations.

Affirmations work best when they are used repeatedly, so the more you read and repeat the affirmation the deeper it reaches and works on your unconscious mind which is the storage centre for all of your self-beliefs.

If for example you were to focus on one affirmation per day begin by clearing your mind and relaxing, then for a minute or two read and repeat the affirmation. When you are saying it, even if it is only in your head, say it with meaning and intention as it will feel more believable this way.

Do this several times a day including first thing in the morning and last thing at night because that is when the mind is most relaxed and receptive as there generally is less interference and background noise from the rest of the world to distract you.

There may be certain affirmations that when you read them you think "Oh that is not me, I am not strong and confident", that is a negative affirmation resurfacing and initially it is normal for this to happen because the negative affirmation is trying to protect itself as your unconscious mind knows that you are attempting to change and replace something. This is called resistance and it is perfectly normal. A classic example of resistance would be if you have ever decided to go on a diet. The minute you use that evil word "Diet" your unconscious protests and starts to tempt you with everything you want to give up. Don't feel bad about it because it happens to us all.

Resistance is a vital part of the way human psychology protects itself but that doesn't mean it cannot be changed, resistance is like a warning making sure that you really want to delete something, think about when you are about to delete a file on your computer, a warning message appears saying "are you sure you want to delete this" your mind works in exactly the same way.

The more you persist the less your unconscious will resist the experience and the change will occur at a deeper level so even if it feels false at first keep practicing them until they feel natural. Any new activity or experience takes a while to become familiar and comfortable and practicing affirmations is no different.

Initially you may not feel like the affirmation you are repeating describes you and that is ok because it is new and like a habit it takes some time to become second nature but essentially the point of the affirmation is to change an existing behaviour or way of relating to yourself and to replace that pattern with a new more positive version. The main thing to remember is that change is possible and with a bit of perseverance you will begin to believe what you are reading and saying.

There is no way to predict how quickly you will notice changes, that will depend entirely on how regularly and how intensely you practice the affirmations but before you get disheartened think about how long you have been repeating negative affirmations, a long time right, maybe even your whole lifetime? It may take a little while to change that programming before a completely new way of relating to yourself can be implemented, just know that they will work if you work them.

Reading affirmations aloud.

Reading your affirmations aloud is useful as it takes a greater degree of effort and concentration, when you read things aloud you tend to read slower and you are more focused on the words you are reading which not only engages your vision but also your hearing thereby activating and engaging more of your senses which will help the affirmation to be absorbed. Again repetition is the key; the more you read it out loud the greater the benefits.

Write down the Affirmation.

Writing down affirmations is a great way to absorb the information because it increases the degree with which you need to concentrate and the greater your concentration the greater the effect of the affirmation. I would suggest taking a full size note pad and each day write and rewrite one affirmation per page. This may take a bit of time but it is well worth it and you will reap the benefit.

While you are writing down the affirmation think about the words and what they mean to you. Imagine yourself becoming the new person described in the affirmation.

Allow yourself to be the person you are describing. Visualise yourself in a new and positive way. This will help you on your journey of transformation and you will also feel that you have accomplished something. Doing this will naturally increase your self-esteem and when the book is completed it will be a real joy to look back and see all of the hard work that you have put into it, plus by the time you have filled the book you should be able to see a real difference in how you relate to yourself.

I think it is also really useful to leave yourself little affirmation notes in drawers and cupboards, they are great to write on post it notes and leave on your wardrobe door or bathroom mirror, inside your purse/wallet or on your fridge because once you have read the affirmation a few times your unconscious will have internalised the words and simply seeing the note will trigger your memory to repeat what is on the note. Again this reinforces the positive message thereby facilitating change at a core level.

Alternatively, and this is a fun way to use affirmations, write each one that you like onto a piece of paper, fold it up and put it in a jar or box then every day choose one at random and allow chance or the universe to guide you on your daily practice. You might be surprised at how appropriate and fitting that day's affirmation is.

Record the Affirmation.

These days most of us have smart phones, camcorders or some other type of recording device.

Record yourself saying the affirmation several times for a minute or two which you can then listen to at your own convenience.

This is a great way to digest the information because you will be more inclined to listen to your own voice which will reinforce your new positive thinking.

It may also be helpful to create a recording for when you go to sleep because your mind will continue to absorb the affirmation as you get into a deeper sleep, this way you are doing the work without actually working.

You can also video yourself saying the affirmations and then watch and repeat back to yourself what you are saying on the video, this way you get a double dose of positivity.

Mirror Work.

It is important to acknowledge and recognise yourself for who you truly are. Far too often people hide from themselves because they have spent years developing a negative body image and have learnt to avoid really looking at themselves and this includes not being able to see yourself at a core level because you believe that you are not good enough.

Mirror work will change that belief because it requires you to confront that misinformed opinion and purposefully look at yourself and I don't mean a passing glance but really sit and look at yourself, to look into your eyes and see the soul that shines brightly within you.

For many people mirror work can be very challenging so if you are new to using affirmations it might be worth starting with the other methods first because you don't want it to be so difficult that you don't use them and then feel worse about yourself.

Mirror work is especially powerful when using Love and Body Image affirmations but it can also be the most challenging. Many people have spent years disliking if not hating themselves so to start saying out loud in front of a mirror that you love yourself can be very difficult but once you get over that initial barrier it can be life changing.

Take five minutes out of your day to practice the following exercise.

Have your affirmation to hand perhaps written down or taped to your mirror where you can see it easily. Spend a moment just looking at yourself, do not judge, comment or belittle yourself, they are soon to be the habits of old.

This is your time to get to know you, to reconnect to the person that has been lost.

Take a minute to look at yourself. Really look at yourself and accept yourself just as you are, regardless of whether you want to change or if you dislike your body, just accept yourself and then start to repeat the affirmation quietly in your head still focusing and looking at yourself. Do this for a couple of minutes, then for the next couple of minutes repeat the affirmation out loud still remaining focused. If you are focusing on a particular part of your body touch and hold the area in question, stroke and soothe yourself as this will help you to link what you are saying to that specific part of your body.

Depending on the affirmation you are saying it can be useful to remove your clothes and accept your naked reflection in the mirror. If this is too difficult the first time then try it in your underwear until you feel comfortable enough to do it without any clothes.

I know this is difficult, it may feel embarrassing and awkward and you may have spent a long time hiding and covering yourself up so reversing that process is going to take some effort. I know this is challenging and I am sure there is a part of you screaming out "I can't do it" and that's ok but it doesn't mean that you give up and don't keep trying.

If you have any body issues this is especially powerful because it can really help you to learn to love and connect to yourself as you are. Ironically the fastest way to change your physical appearance is to first accept it. As difficult as this is it will get easier the more you do it.

If at first this feels too exposing or you feel too vulnerable you could use a handheld mirror and focus on a specific part of your body. If you use this method then you can amend the affirmation to reflect the area you are working on.

For example. *"I AM beautiful/handsome and I love and accept my arms as they are right now"* You can change the word arms to legs, breasts, face etc.

Being able to stand naked in front of a mirror and truly see yourself as you are and accepting your body and saying that you love yourself is one of the most liberating and empowering things you can do.

*

Affirmations are a wonderful way to make changes in your life whether your intention is to build your confidence or self-esteem, to change your relationship with food and your diet, or to find and feel love in your life.

In order for affirmations to really work and have an effect at a core level it will take a degree of dedication on your part. It is important to build affirmation work into your life even it if is just for five minutes in the morning and five minutes in the evening and occasionally throughout the day when you have a spare moment. Affirmations really help to balance and counteract that negative voice that pops up and tells you that you can't do it, that you will never get that job and the person who you really like is never going to be attracted to you.

The more you use affirmations the more effective they will be and the quicker you will start to see changes and results because you really can change your life by changing the words that follow" I AM" so I wish you well on your journey and I will let you begin.

*

"I AM"

Affirmations to improve Self-esteem.

*

I have divided this book into specific categories each one dealing with a particular facet of your life. I have chosen to start with self-esteem because self-esteem can be so fragile and easily damaged however the human race has such an amazing capacity to heal and mend itself.

Regardless of how much or how little self-esteem you have you can always improve and strengthen it. By using affirmations you can intrinsically change how you feel about yourself and your place in the world because the more self-esteem you have the greater your capacity will be to experience happiness and joy.

Self-esteem like confidence determines how you relate to yourself but also how other people relate to you so it is vitally important that you believe in yourself and project that self-belief out into the world in a positive way.

It doesn't matter what you have lived through, what you have experienced you can heal from the inside out and you can start that process by having unshakeable, unbreakable and untouchable self-esteem, all you have to do is believe in yourself. I know that is not easy to do especially if you do not yet believe in yourself but day by day step by step affirmation by affirmation you will get there and you can do it.

All you have to do is trust in the process even if you don't yet trust in yourself.

Repeat each affirmation 10 times before you move on to the next one.

1.

"I AM 100% my authentic self and I AM happy just the way I AM"

2.

"I AM kind and compassionate and I have a lot to offer the world"

3.

"I AM the best person that I can be right now this very minute and I love and accept myself wholeheartedly"

4

"I AM Happy, healthy and full of joy and I have a lot of love to share with the world"

5.

"I AM personally powerful and I AM strong and confident in all that I do"

6.

"I AM honest and truthful and I only associate with other people who are honest and truthful and have my best interests at heart"

7.

"I AM alive and full of vitality, I make the most of everyday because life is a beautiful gift and I intend to enjoy every minute of it"

8.

"I AM unstoppable, Unbeatable, Unfaltering, Unflappable, Undefinable, In fact I AM simply AMAZING"

9.

"I AM always open to new possibilities and opportunities and I welcome and embrace change into my life"

10.

"I AM in control of my thoughts and my actions and I take responsibility for myself and my life"

11.

"I AM calm, patient and tolerant because love and acceptance flows through me today and every day"

12.

"I AM aware that everything that happens to me does so for my benefit and happens in order to teach me a valuable lesson"

13.

"I AM precious, I AM unique, I AM an individual, I AM strong and confident, I AM proud of who I AM and I love and accept myself every day"

14.

"I AM truly blessed with everything that I already have in my life and I give thanks and gratitude"

15.

"I AM in charge of my choices and every day I create the life I want for myself".

16.

"I AM who I want to be and I am a product of my own design"

17.

"I AM strong and confident, I have overcome many difficulties in my life but this has only made me a stronger better person"

18.

"I AM start, intelligent, fun, sexy, loveable, caring, considerate and a good person, I love and appreciate myself for who I AM"

19.

"I AM special because there is only ever going to be one of me and that makes me a unique gift to the world and I celebrate my individuality"

20.

"I AM confident and courageous and nothing can hold me back because I have a strong sense of self and I believe in me"

*

Whatever happens in your life remember that you are capable of dealing with it. Think about all that you have already overcome and know that you can tackle the next obstacle and you can do it with your head held high.

Use these affirmations to build your self-esteem, let it sky rocket and grow taller than any tree or building. Watch it soar into the sky like a bird and allow yourself to be the person you know exists within you unencumbered by fear or doubt.

When you have strong self-esteem there is no limit you cannot reach, no job that you cannot do, no mountain you cannot climb regardless of how difficult it is because you will believe in yourself enough to persevere and keep going.

*

I AM

A Good Person Affirmations.

*

How you THINK about yourself determines how you FEEL about yourself!

How you FEEL about yourself determines how you RELATE to yourself!

When you combine how you think feel and relate to yourself you determine the degree of happiness, joy, love, health, success and prosperity you have in your life.

The relationship you have with yourself is the most important and powerful relationship you will ever experience so you need to like, love and accept yourself as you are this minute so that you can live the best life possible.

For many people who lack self-esteem this can be a very slippery slope into an unhealthy dislike for oneself which can lead to depression, addiction and destructive relationships and even suicidal thoughts and actions.

Often times how we relate to ourselves is a learned experience. I am sure you have seen how some children are taught to dislike themselves because they are subjected to cruel words and violent actions. This leaves the child feeling responsible and to blame believing they are not good enough and that they are undeserving of love. To a child this is the only explanation they can comprehend as to why they are being treated badly by the ones they love the most and who are supposed to love and protect them unconditionally.

As an adult you hopefully realise and learn that being treated badly as a child was not your fault but this is only an intellectual understanding. Emotionally and spiritually there will still be a lingering belief that you are not good enough because why else would those things have happened to you.

This is a normal but unhealthy response because you are not responsible for what happened when you were younger and certainly not responsible for how you were raised and what your parents/family did or said or taught you. I believe that changing the way you think and relate to your past can modify those feeling.

Affirmations speak directly to the unconscious part of brain which is responsible for your beliefs and by changing those thought patterns you can make fundamental changes to your psyche which change how you relate to yourself and your understanding of your place in the world.

Before you can learn to love yourself, respect yourself and have confidence in yourself you need to believe that you are worthy of those things and the only way that is achievable is to learn to believe that you are a good person because when you believe you are a good person you will start to feel deserving of a better life and a desire is created within you that allows and expects to receive the best from life.

The following affirmations are focused on a very simple yet specific message so however you use these affirmations please do not skip over them quickly. Take your time and allow them to become a part of who you are. Practice them with feeling and emotion, you may find it a struggle initially;

you may want to reject and disbelieve the statements but stick with it, remember you are worth it.

You may even find that just by saying these simple affirmations you stir up a lot of emotions and unresolved issues and that is ok because it means that you are starting to make fundamental changes within yourself. It also means that these words are striking a chord with a real unconscious belief.

Again repeat each affirmation 10 times before moving on to the next one and at a later time it may be a good idea to write out each one several times in order to reinforce the new belief.

21.

"I AM a good person and I like myself"

22.

"I AM a good person and I value myself"

23.

"I AM a good person and I accept myself"

24.

"I AM a good person and I love myself"

25.

"I AM a good person and I respect myself"

26.

"I AM a good person and I appreciate myself"

27.

"I AM a good person and I am honest with myself and everyone in my life"

28.

"I AM a good person and I appreciate all that I am and all that I will ever be"

29.

"I AM a good person and I am capable of achieving anything I put my mind to"

30.

"I AM a good person and I am my own best friend"

*

It is important to remember and know that you are a good person. This is the axis on which self-esteem and self-belief rests.

If you have not grown up believing in yourself and your abilities knowing that you are a good person then these affirmations may prove challenging at first but regardless of whether you initially believe them or not please persevere and continue to repeat them until they become a part of your new positive programming.

When you feel resistance don't hesitate, don't stop, instead know that it is a good thing because it means whatever you are saying is having a profound effect on an unconscious level because if it wasn't having an effect it wouldn't be triggering your inner defence mechanisms.

Push through your barriers and defences and allow yourself to feel the true beauty, strength and purity that exist within you. When you believe this you open yourself up to a world that is infinitely happier and you will find that happiness originates from deep within you.

Just remember to tell yourself on a daily basis that YOU ARE A GOOD PERSON.

*

"I AM"

Confidence Affirmations.

*

Affirmations to build your confidence are necessary because no matter who you are or whatever you do there will be at least one area of your life where your confidence is not as strong as it is in other areas whether that be professionally or personally.

These affirmations will help you to feel stronger and more confident in yourself and who you really are.

They will improve your ability to make decisions and choices that are beneficial to you which in turn creates a stronger and more resonant sense of confidence.

Self Confidence affects how you relate to yourself and others but it also affects how other people relate to you. By improving your self-esteem and confidence it can have a ripple effect throughout every area of your life including how friends and family relate and treat you.

You can't expect other people to change or to change how they treat you when you haven't changed.

Remember everything starts with YOU and that includes how you allow other people to treat you. It is your responsibility to set and maintain healthy boundaries.

The more confident you become the more people will notice that there is something different about you. You will start to feel stronger and happier in yourself. You will feel more able to make decisions, to say NO when you need to without fear of rejection or retaliation and even in social situations people will notice that you carry yourself differently.

Confidence will help you to get what you want out of life and to fully love life because you will have the ability to put yourself first for a change and say what it is you really want but more importantly you will be able to speak up and say what you DO NOT want. You will also feel able to change and improve the things that are not working in your life.

There are many ways to practice affirmations but I find listening to a recording of your voice saying these particular affirmations produces amazing results.

It doesn't matter if you choose to repeat one affirmation or a group of them, but listening to yourself saying how confident you are and saying it with real conviction will help your unconscious mind to shift your beliefs and to accept and incorporate what you are saying into your everyday life.

Repeating each affirmation for at least one minute per day several times a day will produce great results especially if you are new to using affirmations or if this is a different way of practicing them.

*

31.

I AM confident in who I AM and what I do.

32.

I AM strong and confident and I have total belief in myself in everything that I do and all that I say"

33.

"I AM confident in myself and my appearance and I stand tall and walk with pride because I project strong confident body language"

34.

"I am confident and courageous in the pursuit of my dreams because I know that I can make them a reality"

35.

"I AM confident in my abilities and it is my responsibility to share my abilities with the rest of the world"

36.

"I AM the most confident person that I can be at this time and I can feel my confidence growing daily"

37.

"I am strong and powerful, I AM fearless and full of confidence, I believe in myself and know that I can achieve anything that I set my mind to, the world is my oyster and nothing is off limits to me"

38.

"I AM confident in my relationships, I set healthy boundaries and I AM able to speak my mind and voice my opinion without fear of rejection"

39.

"I AM confident in all social situations, I enjoy meeting new people and going to new places and people like me for who I AM because I AM a good person"

40.

"I AM confident that I can create the life I want according to my needs and desires and I can achieve that by making smart confident choices"

*

Increasing your confidence is a process but the more you practice affirming your confidence the faster and the stronger it will grow.

When you feel confident in yourself and your abilities you will be able to achieve greater success, you will find the strength to speak your mind and make sure that your voice is heard and that you are living the life you want for yourself rather than accepting the life that someone else deems appropriate for you.

For many people social interaction can create a lot of anxiety, but that anxiety is based in fear because it is conditional to what other people think of you or more importantly what you think other people are going to think of you which is not always accurate because you can never really know what other people are actually thinking.

It took me a long time to understand and realise that just because someone was looking at me it didn't mean they were thinking negatively or criticising me. I was projecting that idea onto other people and then believing my thoughts were their thoughts, when in reality I had no idea what they were thinking. This is a psychological process called "projection" and it is something that everyone does to varying degrees. The important thing is to realise you are doing it so that you can first stop, and then centre yourself and correct your thinking.

Chances are they either not thinking about you at all or they are thinking something positive, it is only your insecurity that convinces you otherwise, and for every one negative comment that you do receive there are probably 100 compliments that you either have refused to accept or have forgotten about.

Building your confidence will flip that around so that you remember every compliment and that one negative comment will no longer hold any importance for you.

The more confident you become the less concerned you will be about the opinions of others and you will be able to fully engage and enjoy what you are doing at that moment and commit to it without fear of external judgement.

I can guarantee that you will have more fun, be more care free and when you are confident in yourself other people will be drawn to you.

Remember in order to build your confidence repetition is the key so keep practicing, keep pushing yourself and never stop believing in YOU.

"I AM"

Affirmations for Success.

*

Everyone wants and needs to feel successful regardless of where you are or what you are doing in your life.

It doesn't matter if you are climbing the corporate ladder or at home with 3 children or a million other options in-between, because whatever you are doing it is important to feel good about it and the best way to feel good about something is to know that you are successful in what you are doing.

Nobody wants to be the worst executive in the world or the worst parent. Of course you want to be good at what you do and you should feel successful because believing you are successful will bring about the success you desire.

If you speak to anyone who has "Made it" whatever that really means they will tell you that they believed in themselves and thought of themselves as successful long before the physical success materialised.

In this sense affirmations are like visualisations.

You need to see and believe something in order for it to become a reality. If you don't believe me just imagine any product that you use whether it be your mobile phone, your car or your hairdryer, somebody had to imagine what the product would do and what it would look like then they had to develop it and figure out how to make it work, but without that spark, without the idea you would still be walking everywhere and sending handwritten letters.

They had to will whatever it is into existence and you have the same ability to do this with your life.

These affirmations are great to say out loud and I recommend saying each one for at least one minute at a time.

If you choose to say them then don't rush it, take your time, say each word with meaning, feel yourself in the affirmation, know that you are successful allow that thought to become a feeling inside your body so that it is tangible and a physical sensation. Allow it to fill you up and take you over.

Say each affirmation slowly with a clear strong voice; make sure your intention is absolute while you are affirming your success.

Another important element of saying "I AM" is that you are affirming something in the present moment in the here and now; it is not about the past or way off in the future.

You are feeling successful now and that will help to change your cognitive state and alter your mood to one that is positive and strong. This feeling will be amplified if you have already been practicing the Confidence Affirmations.

You will find that each section naturally evolves and builds upon the previous one, like building a house, you start with the foundations and add one brick after another until it is completed and you are exactly the same, you must continue to "add" to your life to develop and grow and to feel happy and valuable as a person.

41.

"I AM successful in everything that I do regardless of the outcome"

42.

"I am capable of turning every negative into a positive situation because I have total belief in myself and my capabilities"

43.

"I AM a success in all that I do because I approach everything with honesty, sincerity and integrity"

44.

"I AM a magnet that attracts prosperity and success into my life and into any project I AM involved with"

45.

"I AM successful in every area of my life because success is a state of mind and my mind is positive and confident"

46.

"I AM successful regardless of the outcome because I AM able to learn from every situation and improve upon it in the future"

47.

"I AM successful because I refuse to accept anything less than the best and because I AM focused 100% on whatever I AM doing"

48.

"I AM happy and fulfilled because I breathe in success and refuse to allow fear and disappointment to hold me back"

49.

"I AM committed to being the best person that I can be at all times and I attract success into my life with positive thoughts and positive actions"

50.

"I am financially, spiritually and emotional wealthy in every area of my life"

*

Remember your success begins with your beliefs and your intentions. The degree of success you feel and achieve is determined by your desire and the strength of your commitment to being successful.

You can achieve anything when you are focused and have the courage of your convictions.

It is important to remember that being successful doesn't necessarily mean earning a lot of money or having the fastest car, you can be successful in writing poetry, keeping your house clean, being a good friend, partner or parent.

Whatever it is you do, make sure that you are successful in how you do it regardless of what it is. You can be a success in any and all areas of your life.

Don't judge or measure your success against what you either perceive success to be or in comparison to someone else's success.

Your success is exactly that, YOURS. Celebrate your abilities your successes and you will feel your self-esteem improve daily.

"If you can dream it you can achieve it."

*

The more you repeat these affirmations the more successful you will feel in all areas of your life and that will create an environment where you are able to create even greater success by taking regular productive action because the more you do the more you will achieve. Affirmations will help bring about success and provide you with the motivation and belief to achieve anything you set your mind to but you must also take action.

Use these affirmations to bring about the success you desire and then feel that success within you before it materialises in the physical realm because all success is visualised before it is actually created.

*

"I AM"

Affirmations for Inner Strength.

*

Nobody is able to navigate their way through life without experiencing difficult times and having to overcome obstacles. Regardless of where you live in the world or your social, financial status you will have to develop an inner strength to get you through the day.

Many people not only have to support themselves emotionally and financially but also their children and families in which case you need to be even stronger than if you only had to worry about yourself.

Ironically inner strength develops from having lived through your trials and tribulations and come through them stronger on the other side. Therefore the stronger you are the more difficulties you will have dealt with in your life and each one prepares you and makes you stronger for the next one, but it never hurts to have a little help along the way or to have a few tricks up your sleeve.

These "Inner Strength" affirmations are precisely the tools that are going to get you through the day when you feel like giving up and staying in bed with the curtains closed and a tub of ice-cream for company.

They are also great reminders of just how strong you truly are and they cover a broad spectrum of your daily life, so if there are particular areas that you need to develop or work on then this will help you to develop and recognise the strength that is already inside you but have yet to tap into.

However you use these affirmations try to inject intention and authority into them, know that you are strong, feel that inner strength that resides deep inside you that is just waiting to be released because you are a WARRIOR.

As with everything else in life the more effort you put into it the greater the reward and that is certainly true when using affirmations.

*

51.

"I AM strong and confident in all that I do and all that I say"

52.

"I AM strong enough to take responsibility for my life and my actions which gives me strength of character and the determination to be the best person I can be"

53.

"I AM strong and beautiful/handsome and I carry myself with dignity and pride"

54.

"I AM strong enough to fight for what I believe in and I believe in MYSELF"

55.

"I AM strong enough to make my dreams a reality because I know that I deserve happiness"

56.

"I AM strong and confident which is why every day I treat myself with love and respect"

57.

"I AM strong and confident in who I am which is why I relinquish the pain of my past and clear a path for a bright and happy future"

58.

"I AM strong enough to learn from my mistakes because I know they make me stronger, wiser and a better person in every way"

59.

"I AM strong and confident and I create healthy boundaries in all areas of my life"

60.

"I AM physically and mentally strong and I can take on every challenge that life presents me with because I AM a Warrior"

*

For many people it is easy to forget just how strong they are or how much they have already overcome and the challenges they have faced fought and won.

Most people are much stronger than they give themselves credit for but by repeating these affirmations and making them a part of your daily routine you will remind yourself just how strong you truly are, you will acknowledge your inner strength and when you feel strong and capable the general trials and tribulations of life will seem so much easier to manage and they will not hold you back or drag you down.

Likewise when you are faced with greater challenges you will already know that you are capable of successfully dealing with them because your confidence, your self-esteem and your belief in yourself will be significantly higher.

Remember to give yourself some credit and praise yourself regularly.

*

"I AM"

Responsibility Affirmations.

*

Being responsible for yourself and your life is a very powerful attribute. Many people try to avoid and deny their responsibility not only to themselves but to others, generally you will find those people are unhappy, angry and play the blame game at every opportunity thinking that everything that has gone wrong in their lives is due to someone else or because of what somebody else has said or done. They absolve themselves of any responsibility because taking responsibility would feel so overwhelming that it is easier to deny it.

Taking responsibility for your life, for you words, for your actions gives you power. It makes you strong, stronger that you can possibly imagine because it means that you are consciously aware of your actions and that can give you clarity and a focus that other people do not have.

Every time you accept responsibility for something you take ownership of it, whether it is your happiness, your financial situation or the amount of love you have in your life, even your wrong doings.

When you take ownership and responsibility you then have the power to change your life in positive ways because you are aware that everything in your life is the way it is because of your actions and your choices and yes you can change those choices and take different actions. If there is an area in your life that is not working for you then you can change it and the fastest way to change it is to take responsibility for it. When you do there will be nothing that you cannot achieve.

Before you start practicing these affirmations, question the extent to which you take responsibility in your own life, ask yourself "Do I play the blame game?"

This is not an exercise in punishment and it is not designed to make you feel guilty for your actions, it is perhaps more of a wakeup call because you cannot change your behaviour unless you first know what your behaviour is.

Being self-aware is the foundation for any and all change because how can you strive for something better when you don't understand why it isn't working in the first place otherwise you will end up repeating the same mistakes again and again.

61.

"I AM responsible for my thoughts and my actions because taking responsibility means I AM in charge of my life and my destiny"

62.

"I AM responsible for everything that happens in my life and I make positive choices in how I respond and deal with what happens in my life"

63.

"I AM responsible for my health and today I will only make healthy choices and give my body the respect it deserves"

64.

"I AM responsible for my relationships and the people that I attract into my life so I choose to only attract people that are positive and have my best interests at heart"

65.

"I AM responsible for creating healthy boundaries and it is my duty to make sure that other people respect those boundaries and I enforce that by respecting those boundaries myself"

66.

"I AM responsible for being the best person that I can be and every day I take positive steps towards that goal"

67.

"I AM responsible for my happiness and only my happiness and it is ok to put myself first and make ME happy"

68.

"I AM responsible for my mistakes and I take ownership of them because I choose to learn and grow from the past in order to create a better future for myself and my family"

69.

"I AM responsible for my actions, my decisions, my words and the intention I inject into every day so that I can be a positive force for good in the world"

70.

"I AM responsible for making today, tomorrow and every day the best day of my life, I AM responsible for my happiness, my health, my wealth and wellbeing. I am grateful for all that I have and all that I have yet to receive and I give thanks every day to a power that is greater than my own"

*

When you take responsibility for your words your actions your life, what you are actually doing is taking control, you regain your personal power by saying I am strong enough to accept what has happened in my life and I can deal with it, fix it or choose never to repeat it again.

Taking responsibility gives you strength.

*

Taking responsibility for your actions makes you powerful.

*

Being responsible with your words makes you compassionate.

*

Accepting responsibility for your thoughts puts you in control.

*

When you have the ability to live this way you become the director of your life and not an extra.

Never forget taking responsibility gives you Power and as famously said in every Spiderman film *"With great power comes great responsibility"*

*

"I AM"

Gratitude Affirmations

*

Gratitude is such an important part of our lives and yet it is so often overlooked. We live in a society that promotes having more and having it now. We have lost, or are losing the ability to sit and simply be, and be happy with where we are now and with what we already have.

There is so much focus on what we don't have and getting more that we don't take enough to time look around and recognise all that is already in our lives and to be grateful for that.

This is why gratitude affirmations play a vital part in changing your whole attitude and approach to life. One of the reasons that we "mankind" is becoming more and more unsatisfied with our lives is because we are always searching for and wanting more.

When you always want something that you haven't got or that is out of reach it creates a feeling of unworthiness and jealousy. You start to look around and see other people with better things or living "better" lives and you start to question what is wrong with you and why haven't got the same things.

Gratitude is something that takes work and time. Some things will be easy to be grateful for while other things will be more difficult but like anything worth having it takes dedication and patience.

Not everyone has lived a blessed life and many of us, in fact most of us myself included have experienced pain and some form of trauma in life that you would probably rather forget, but rather than focusing on the negative things in life gratitude allows you to live in the light, to find the best in all things, to open your soul and allow purity to enter and connect to the "here and now".

Take a moment to look around you and see all that you already have, not what you think you don't have, and if that feels difficult to do at first be grateful that you have eyes to see and other senses that allow you to experience the world, start with the basics such as your senses or your body and what it enables you to do.

When you start to practice gratitude what feels like your worst day can still have purpose and meaning because amongst the stress of it you can always find something to be grateful for and if you struggle with that be grateful that you had a tough day because it means you are still alive and that in itself is something to be thankful for.

Make saying gratitude affirmations a daily habit until it becomes second nature and then see how different your day looks.

Living a life of gratitude means being connected to something other than yourself because it is not about your ego or your emotional state, it transcends emotion into something more untouchable and beautiful.

Why not start a daily gratitude list or a gratitude diary and use the following affirmations as a source of inspiration.

*

71.

"I AM thankful because my life is abundant with many wonderful things for which I am truly grateful"

72.

"I AM grateful every day that I am alive and have an opportunity to start again and make the best of today and every day"

73.

"I AM alive and full of gratitude because I know that I am blessed and I was put on this earth to be happy and share happiness"

74.

"I AM grateful for all that I have and all that I am yet to receive"

75.

"I AM grateful for all that the universe bestows upon me and I know that everything that comes to me does so at the right time in the right way"

76.

"I AM grateful for the strength to rise above any difficult situation the universe presents to me because I know it is an opportunity to grow and develop as a person"

77.

"I AM grateful for every trial and tribulation that I have survived and overcome because my past has made me a stronger, wiser and better person"

78.

"I AM grateful to everyone who has ever touched my heart and for all the love that I have in my life because I am surrounded by love"

79.

"I AM grateful for my health and my ability to do all that I can do" (it is important to repeat this regardless of the state of your health)

80.

"I AM grateful for my freedom, for my ability to think and speak freely and to express myself without fear of repercussions"

81.

"I am truly grateful for all of the bad times because they made the good times so much sweeter"

*

Have you ever heard the saying Money attracts Money" well the same can be said for gratitude because the more gratitude you feel and express the more you will find you have to be grateful for, not only that but you will start to realise that there was so much already in your life that you were previously blind to.

No matter what, every day you have a reason to be grateful, it may be the worst day of your life and even then you can be grateful because if it's the worst day of your life then it cannot get any worse.

Gratitude is a state of mind and the more you are grateful the greater sense of peace you will find within yourself and the more you will have to smile about every day and that can have a positive effect on those around you which is one more reason to be grateful.

*

"I AM"

Health and Diet Affirmations.

*

Our health and our diet is such an integral part of our lives yet so often it is overlooked and taken for granted. We push our bodies too hard and I don't mean at the gym. We eat too much, and eat too much of the wrong food, we drink too much, smoke too much and even if you do not smoke air pollution is an issue for anyone who lives in or near a city. We don't get enough sleep and that combined with a lack of the right nutrients has a significant effect on our productivity our positivity our objectivity and our general ability to perform and function as the vital human beings we are supposed to be (that is assuming that you are already in good or reasonable physical health)

If you have an existing medical conditions or ailment maintaining a positive attitude is of even greater importance because your mental health has a direct correlation with your physical health. So a positive mental attitude will have positive physical effects in the same way that a negative mental attitude will drain and deplete your body.

It is also important to have a healthy relationship with food which for many people is proving to be more and more of a struggle. We live in a society that dictates what you should look like, what size and shape you should be and if you don't fit into that ideal then you simply don't fit in. This is a cause of many eating disorders and food related issues whether it is under or over eating, binging or self-imposed starvation.

Although affirmations can be a valuable tool in food and health management if you are concerned about your relationship to food you should seek professional help from your doctor or a specialist.

It is important to have a positive attitude towards your heath and diet and it is even more important to feel that they are under your control.

I have created the following affirmations to help keep a positive and balanced view around health and diet and have purposefully not included affirmations promoting either weight loss or weight gain because used in the wrong context or intention can be more destructive than constructive.

These affirmations are designed to help you feel positive and in control of your health in a balanced and stable fashion, however if you make changes to your diet chances are you will experience similar changes in your weight or your body.

82.

"I AM in control of my health and my diet and I make healthy choices that are good for me"

83.

"I AM abundant with good health and optimism and I can feel vitality and energy flowing through me"

84.

"I AM in control of what I eat and I only eat healthy food that nourishes my mind and my body"

85.

"I AM in control of what I eat and I will only eat when I am physically hungry and stop when I am full.

86.

"I am fit and healthy and I love and appreciate my body"

87.

(If you are suffering from a medical condition or problem then please fill in the blank with the name of the illness or problem. This will make it more relevant and personal for you and will instruct your body to heal the specific area)

*"I AM strong and healthy and my (*fill in the blank*) is healing from the inside out and it is getting better every day"*

88.

"I AM getting stronger and healthier every day in every way."

89.

"I AM strong vibrant and healthy because my mind is strong and healthy and I breathe in all of the positivity the universe has to offer me"

90.

"I am in control of my appetite and my desires and I make healthy food choices and positive decisions"

91.

"I AM pain free, I AM unrestricted in my movement, I AM happy, I AM strong, I AM me"

92.

"I AM who I AM and I accept myself, my body and my situation as it is right now but I know that I AM improving on a daily basis"

93.

"I inhale good health and positivity and exhale illness disease and negativity leaving my body cleansed and in perfect health"

*

No matter what your physical condition is, your mental state will influence how your body reacts and recovers therefore it is important to always remain positive.

Many people have illnesses and ailments that are permanent and lifelong but how you choose to deal with those issues will impact the quality of your life. If you walk around complaining every day you are only going to feel down and depressed about your situation which will make the problem seem even worse than it is.

For example, I have a friend who for the last few years has had several serious medical conditions and has been in a wheelchair for the last two years. When I saw her recently she said "This has been two years into my life not two years out of my life" and that really moved me and only confirmed that how you think about your circumstances determines how you create your reality.

I am not suggesting that affirmations are going to miraculously cure any illness or disease but they will help you manage those conditions and how you cope with them.

Likewise practicing diet affirmations will help to change your mind set and create healthier boundaries in relation to food or even addictions such as drugs and alcohol.

You have the power to make healthy choices in order to create the best possible life for yourself. You can change your thinking and your relationship to food. Changing your perspective and how you think about your diet and losing weight will change the relationship you have with it.

Instead of thinking about going on a diet change that idea to only eating healthily, it will remove the pressure of dieting but still have the same physical effect of losing weight but without the negative connotations. If you have ever been on a diet you will know that the minute you make that decision you become permanently hungry and start craving everything that you have promised not to eat.

Practicing positive affirmations will help you change your perspective and that will change your thinking and that will produce positive changes in your body.

Remember it's your life and you have the power to create it anyway you see fit.

"I AM"

Love Affirmations.

*

We all deserve, need and crave love. We need to love and respect ourselves as well as feeling loved and respected by others.

I believe the best way to express love to others is by developing and learning the capacity to love yourself.

Some people think it is selfish and narcissistic to love yourself but I am not talking about a vain shallow exterior form of love where you spend forever looking in the mirror.

I am referring to a genuine deep and true love and respect for yourself that many people have never managed to develop or were never taught to develop because their teachers (namely their parents) did not love or know how to love themselves, and unfortunately as is so often the case because they either lack the capacity or ability they were unable to teach their children how to love themselves. Instead and rather regrettably they were taught how not to love themselves.

When you don't know how to love yourself it is very hard to create healthy boundaries in your life because you put the needs of others before your own and often times to the detriment of you own health happiness and wellbeing.

I see people all the time who do not love themselves, it shows in how they carry themselves, in the things they say about themselves and others, it shows in the unhealthy and abusive relationships they cling onto. I see it in the way they talk to and treat their children, partners, family members and acquaintances.

For many people their own self-worth is tied up in love or the idea of love. They believe that being single means that they are unlovable but this is only an indication of a lack of self-love.

Likewise for some people being in a bad or abusive relationship is preferable to not being in a relationship at all and this may be a learned pattern of behaviour that developed as a child or later as an adult. But again only someone who does not know how to love themselves would allow someone else to treat them badly. If this speaks to you directly and you find it upsetting I apologise but the fact that you are responding emotionally means that what I am saying has connected with you on an emotional level and that will make these affirmations all the more important to you.

There are of course different type of love, there is the love we have for oneself, for our friends family, children and of course romantic love. Regardless of your current situation it is important to feel love, if not from others then from yourself.

I know for some people this is especially hard which is why I have left this section until the end of the book. It may be difficult to say the words "I love myself" and if that is true of you then I urge you to say it as often as you can because the more you say it the greater the likelihood is that you will start to believe it and when you believe it you will feel it at a core level and when that happens it will change your life.

For those who find this difficult I have a process that may help.

Start off but saying the affirmation in your head but imagine yourself saying it as a whisper. Repeat this for at least one minute several times a day for one week.

Then say it in a normal voice (again still in your head) repeat for one week.

Then shout it out at the top of your voice, (still in your head) again for one week.

As each week passes is should get easier and you should feel more comfortable saying the affirmation.

Now repeat the same process out loud. Start off with a whisper and progress saying it louder and louder. (You don't have to shout it out at the top of your voice unless you want to or if you live in the middle of a field.) I wouldn't want your neighbours to think that you have lost your mind.

As mentioned at the beginning of this book there are several ways to use affirmations and for Love Affirmations especially I recommend you use every method.

Record yourself saying "I AM loveable and I love myself", write it on post it notes that you leave in every room of your house. Have a note pad where you write in down. Get used to seeing and hearing those 3 words.

Mirror work is also beneficial for these affirmations but depending on just how much you struggle with this particular affirmation it may be worth leaving the mirror work near to the end of the process. Try each method individually for a week at a time in order to see what you feel is most beneficial for you. It may be that afterward you use a combination of techniques but as long as it works for you that's what counts.

Affirmations are useful in attracting romantic love also. Like the law of attraction: what you project out into the world is what you in turn receive so thinking and believing that you deserve love will help to bring it into your life.

I know that many people desire a relationship because they need to feel loved but I believe it is more important to start learning to love yourself first. If you do this I can guarantee that suddenly you will start to attract more love into your life and the quality of the person you attract will also improve, this is because you are relating to yourself in a healthier fashion and so the universe will mirror that by bringing you more stable and equal relationships. When you love yourself you will no longer be prepared to settle for anything or anyone less than you deserve.

With that said I truly hope that these affirmations bring you all that you desire and you allow their power to work wonders in your life.

94.

"I AM awash with love because it fills and flows through me every day"

95.

"I AM lovely and loveable and I deserve to love and be loved"

96.

"I AM worthy of love, not just love but true and deep love that touches my soul and touches the soul of others"

97.

"My heart is open and ready to receive love"

98.

"I AM allowed to love myself and I make a choice to love and accept myself as I AM"

99.

"I AM inviting love and positivity into my life every day and love carries me through the darkness and illuminates my path"

100.

"I AM deserving of unlimited and unwavering love and affection.

101.

"I AM a loving and giving person and I radiate positivity and joy which attracts love, positivity and joy back into my life"

*

It's important to feel loved but it is even more important to love yourself.

Practice loving yourself every day. Use these affirmations by building them into your life but go beyond just saying affirmations and start living them by taking positive action.

Using affirmations is a great way to attract love into your life however if you stay at home and never go out it doesn't matter how much love you attract into your life because you will never be able to actualise it. You must create the opportunity for love to find you. It is very unlikely that the next guy who delivers your pizza will be the love of your life. If he is that's great and I am happy for you, especially if you get free chicken wings but all joking aside, just like everything else in life if you really want something you have to go and get it or make it happen and finding love really is no different.

Additionally start doing little things for yourself that show love. Appreciate yourself. Treat yourself to something special as you might treat your lover or partner. It's amazing how we can put other people's needs before our own and we will go out of our way to do something nice for someone else; well you need to start doing that for yourself. You are important to you know.

When your heart is open your capacity to fill it with love multiplies exponentially whether that is love for yourself, those around you or someone new.

*

Well that brings us to the end of 101 "I AM Power Affirmation and I hope you have enjoyed them and that they help you to be the best version of yourself that you can be and become the architect in your life.

Never forget that affirmations have the power to change your thinking how you feel about yourself, your relationship with yourself and others, therefore just one of these affirmations can have a profound and life changing effect. I therefore hope that this collection of 101 Affirmations not only finds a place in your life but also in your heart and soul.

I truly believe that practice makes perfect and the more you work at "affirming" what you desire the more they will work for you. I know I have said it before but repetition really is the key.

Repeating an affirmation once or twice here and there is not going to bring about much of a change in your life. In order for them to work you have to do the work.

I always advise people to build affirmations into their daily routine starting first thing in the morning and throughout the day and last thing at night before you go to sleep.

Starting your day with positive affirming thoughts is equivalent to eating a healthy breakfast. It sets you up for the day, it puts a spring in your step and creates the right frame of mind to go forth and be productive positive and prosperous.

Whatever affirmations you use in whichever way you use them I hope they bring about a positive and profound change in your life but remember the more you use them the greater effect they will have and never forget what you **affirm you confirm.**

Sending you love and positivity.

Tony T.

And now for a bonus.

For anyone interested in having an extra Confidence Boost I have included the first 10 quotes from my book "101 Confidence Quotes that will change your life". I am especially proud of this book and think the quotes in this book can really have a life changing effect in building your confidence. I hope they also motivate and inspire you as they have so many other people.

101

Confidence Quotes

That will change your life.

1.

Right now, this very second you are the best that you can be because you cannot be anything other than what you are. Celebrate yourself. Love yourself. Respect yourself. Accept yourself. Trust yourself. Have faith in yourself and know that you are a good person.

2.

Greatness is achieved by overcoming challenges and by pushing yourself to do things you didn't know that you could do but believed in yourself enough to try. Nothing rewarding ever came without effort. Try and if that doesn't work try again, then try harder. Remember that you are worth the effort.

3.

You are the living embodiment of Ultimate Hope, Pure Love and Infinite Possibilities. You can do anything when you apply yourself and have faith in your abilities. Never give up. Never back down. Stay strong and know that you can do it.

4.

If you follow someone else's path you will end up at their destination. Follow your dreams; listen to where your heart is calling you to go. Enjoy your journey and find your own destination, you owe it to yourself to fulfil the destiny that is rightfully yours.

5.

I have found that the people who accuse you of being selfish are only doing so because you are not doing what they want, when they want, in the way they want you to do it and if that makes you selfish then so be it because really they are the ones who are being selfish for expecting you to meet their demands and needs ahead of your own. Don't feel guilty, don't feel bad about yourself instead realise that they are trying to manipulate you for their own interests, to fulfil their needs; they are not concerned by what you want or need, so ask yourself who is being selfish and who is letting who down?

6.

We all need validation, for someone to tell us that we are doing well, that we are doing the right thing and are on the right path. The problem is we look for that validation in the wrong place. We seek external validation from friends, family, teachers etc, but we need to turn that need inwards and validate ourselves. We need to trust our own instincts and know what we are doing is the right thing for ourselves. We also need to congratulate and applaud ourselves for our achievements. Yes it is nice to receive recognition from other people but let that be the icing on the cake. You need to be the cake. You are the foundation. You need to believe it first otherwise you give far too much power to other people who may not always have your best interests at heart and if you do not really believe in yourself when you receive compliments from other people you will be incapable of accepting it. Love and trust yourself first and confidence will flow through you.

7.

The best investment you will ever make is in YOURSELF, never forget that you are worth the effort. Every struggle you endure today will benefit you tomorrow and in the future. Eat right, exercise often, believe in yourself, push yourself harder than yesterday, do what scares you, give of yourself willingly and watch the quality of your life improve daily. When you love and respect yourself you will receive love and respect from others. Prove to yourself and the world just how valuable you truly are.

8.

Every day is an opportunity to start again, to wipe the slate clean, to forget the mistakes and disappointments of yesterday and to move on, it is an opportunity to make new decisions, implement new plans, start new healthy habits, create boundaries and allow positivity and love into your life. You can be who you want to be, you can do what you want to do. You do not have to be restricted or defined by previous actions. You are in control of your life, you are in control of your actions and that means you have the ultimate power over your life just make sure that you are living it your way and to the best of your ability.

9.

In life you are guaranteed to get it wrong, to make mistakes, hurt the ones you love, fall, fail and feel fed up but that doesn't mean that you give up. You shake it off, learn from it and grow as a person so that you make less and less mistakes in the future. Remember what is a negative today can be turned into a positive tomorrow.

10.

Don't cry for the person that you used to be. Thank them because without them you couldn't be the beautiful strong person that you are today. We are all evolving and must shed the skin of our yesterdays in order to blossom into who we are supposed to be today.

*

Thank you for taking the time to read my book and to allow me to share my thoughts and ideas with you as well as affirmations that I use and have used throughout my life.

Once again thank you.

Tony T.

95873747R00049

Made in the USA
Columbia, SC
16 May 2018